Favorite
CLASSICAL Melodies

F HORN

Arranged and Recorded by David Pearl
("Brandenburg Concerto No. 5, First Movement" arranged and recorded by Donald Sosin)

Cherry Lane Music Company
Director of Publications/Project Supervisor: Mark Phillips

ISBN: 978-1-60378-409-2

Visit our website at www.cherrylaneprint.com

CONTENTS

AVE MARIA

TRACK 1

HORN

By Charles Gounod and Johann Sebastian Bach

Moderately slow

Piano

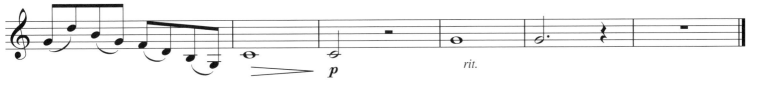

BRANDENBURG CONCERTO NO. 5,
FIRST MOVEMENT

By Johann Sebastian Bach

F HORN

CARO MIO BEN

HORN

By Giuseppe Giordani

Moderately slow

CLAIR DE LUNE

By Claude Debussy

HORN

Slowly

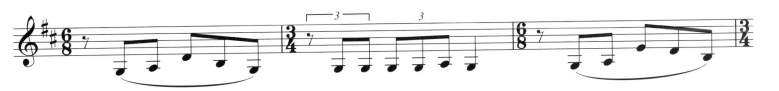

FUNERAL MARCH OF A MARIONETTE

HORN

by Charles Gounod

Moderately fast, in 2

GYMNOPÉDIE NO. 1

HORN

By Erik Satie

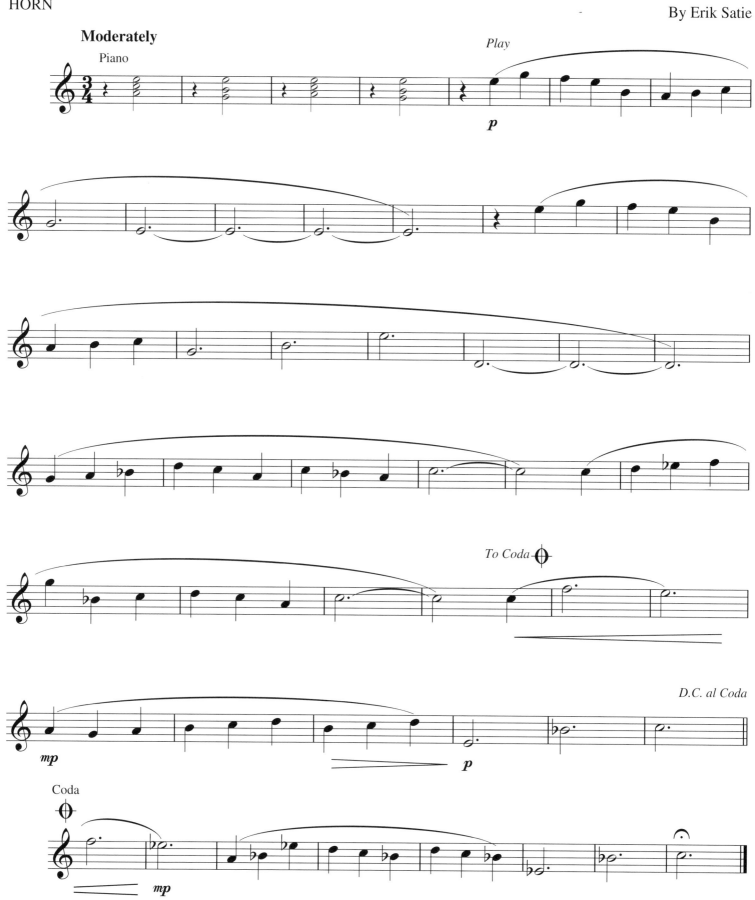

HALLELUJAH CHORUS

from *Messiah*

By George Frideric Handel

HORN

Moderately fast

Piano

Play

HUNGARIAN DANCE NO. 5

HORN

By Johannes Brahms

Moderately

Slower

Tempo I

MINUET
(from String Quintet in E Major)

HORN

By Luigi Boccherini

Moderately

PIANO SONATA NO. 14 "MOONLIGHT"

First Movement

HORN

By Ludwig van Beethoven

SYMPHONY NO. 5

First Movement

HORN

By Ludwig van Beethoven

WILLIAM TELL OVERTURE

HORN

By Gioacchino Rossini

Moderately fast

POMP AND CIRCUMSTANCE

TRACK 13

HORN

By Edward Elgar